Weldon

Weldon

Contributions:

-Officer Surowiec, School Resource Officer, Gwinnett County Schools Police

-Officer Stewart, School Resource Officer, Gwinnett County Schools Police

-Anonymous Instagram Users

Inspiration for this book comes from my friends and family in law enforcement, as well as my good friend Yohnny who is also writing a book and sparked the idea for Chaos Explained.

Weldon

Ebook ISBN: 978-1-716-03360-5

Imprint: Lulu.com

25% of the profit from the sale of this product will be donated to the (NLEOMF) National Law Enforcement Officer Memorial Fund.

Cover Art Designed by Zachary Weldon with Canva.com

Weldon

Dedication:

This book is dedicated to all of our brave first responders. More specifically, this book is dedicated to those who have died in the line of duty. Thank you for your sacrifice. You are not Forgotten. As the Bible says in the Book of John, chapter 15, verse 13, "Love has nothing greater than this, that one would die for his friends." As a way to pay back the sacrifices made by these brave individuals, 25% of the profit from this product will be donated to the National Law Enforcement Officer Memorial Fund.

Weldon

Police Officers Oath:

"On my honor, I will never Betray my integrity, my character, Or the public trust. I will always have the courage to hold myself and others accountable for our actions. I will always maintain the highest ethical standards and uphold the values of my community, and the agency I serve."

About- This book explains what happens, why it happens, and the other possible outcomes of Police Incidents. As well as teachings of police and for police. I wrote this book to discuss the current climate of policing and views of law enforcement. I also wanted to teach others some things in policing that could help them form a view on the subject.

Acknowledgments

Thank you to all of the people who supported my efforts in writing this book. A huge part of the print and publication was those who believed in me.

Thank you to all our brave Law Enforcement Officers as well as any other first responders that keep their communities safe. You are greatly appreciated. May God bless you and your families.

Thank you to the mentors from my life that taught me the information used to write this book. I would not be where I am today if it was not for them.

"If you can't make them see the light, make them feel the heat" -Former U.S. President, Ronald Reagan.

Chaos Explained

Weldon

Chaos Explained

Law Enforcement Explained

Written By: Zachary T. Weldon

Table of Contents

Table of Contents cont...

What is Going On?

Hi, my name is Zachary Weldon and I am a Law Enforcement Explorer in the State of Georgia. I am 15 years old and take Defensive Tactics classes regularly. I take Use of Force Classes and have a wide knowledge of Law Enforcement. I write this to discuss what happened mainly throughout 2020 and some events prior when it comes to Law Enforcement. I have studied the events that we will discuss in the book, I have done my research.

The information given will be completely unbiased and purely from my research and none of my opinions will be found here without context. I also interview multiple people to gain new points of view that some people might skip over. I interview people from the police officers that are at my school to random people I found on social media. I also gather information from both sides of the spectrum. I interview people who support law enforcement, as well as people who do not support them, and then all the way to people who haven't chosen sides because simply just don't know what to think about it.

Please keep in mind that this is not meant to support either side of the ongoing conflict of supporting or not supporting law enforcement. This is informational writing meant to inform and educate people on these subjects. While I do support law enforcement, I respect people's opinions and don't get worked up over the views that you are entitled to.

Weldon

What is a Law Enforcement Officer?

There are multiple appropriate titles for a Law Enforcement Officer. If you see these throughout the writing you know what they mean. There are Law Enforcement Officer, Police Officer, Peace Officers, Safety Officers, Public Servant, Public Service agents, Officer, and policemen. There are also inappropriate titles for them as well. There are Fuzz, Pig, Twelve, Bootlicker, and Gestapo. These are all the terms or titles given to officers by the public and their departments. While some of them are good in terms of meaning, some can be offensive or extremely rude.

The first thing I want to talk about is, what exactly is a Police Officer and what is their job? Law Enforcement Officers (LEOs) do more than just; sit in speed traps, give tickets, shoot people, and take people to jail. They work holidays, the work deaths and homicides, they save lives through means of CPR when someone stops breathing, they respond to home invasion calls, they protect their communities, and are the reason that the crime rates are as low as they are. The Law Enforcement Oath is,

"On my honor, I will never Betray my integrity, my character, or the public trust. I will always have the courage to hold myself and others accountable for our actions. I will always maintain the highest ethical standards and uphold the values of my community, and the agency I serve."

Every officer on duty has taken that oath and while some do break it, most do not. Studies show that less than %0.5 of officers are corrupt. Out of roughly 800,000 sworn officers in the U.S., that leaves us with around 4,000 corrupt officers. I am about to provide a poem for you that was written by a man named Paul Harvey.

Paul Harvey: "Policeman"

"A Policeman is a composite of what all men are, mingling of a saint and sinner, dust and deity.

Gulled statistics wave the fan over stinkers, underscore instances of dishonesty and brutality because they are 'news'. What they really mean is that they are exceptional, they are unusual, they are not commonplace.

Buried under the froth is the fact, and the fact is that: Less than one-half of one percent of policemen misfit the uniform and that is a better average than you'd find among clergymen.

Weldon

What is a policeman? He, of all men, is once the most needed and the most unwanted. A strangely nameless creature who is "sir" to his face and "pig" or worse behind his back.

He must be such a diplomat that he can settle differences between individuals so that each will think he won. But…If the policeman is neat, he's conceited; if he's careless, he's a bum. If he's pleasant, he's a flirt; if he's not, he's a grouch.

He must make an instant decision which would require months for a lawyer to make.

But…If he hurries, he's careless; if he's deliberate, he's lazy. He must be first to an accident and infallible with his diagnosis. He must be able to start breathing, stop bleeding, tie splints and, above all, be sure the victim goes home without a limp. Or expect to be sued.

The police officer must know every gun, draw on the run, and hit where it doesn't hurt. He must be able to whip two men twice his size and half his age without damaging his uniform and without being "brutal". If you hit him, he's a coward. If he hits you, he's a bully.

A policeman must know everything-and not tell. He must know where all the sin is and not partake.

Weldon

A policeman must, from a single human hair, be able to describe the crime, the weapon, the criminal- and tell you where the criminal is hiding.

But…If he catches the criminal, he's lucky; if he doesn't, he's a dunce. If he gets promoted, he has political pull; if he doesn't, he's a dullard. The policeman must chase a bum lead to a dead-end, stake out ten nights to tag one witness who saw it happen but refuses to remember.

He runs files and writes reports until his eyes ache, to build a case against some felon who will get 'dealed out' by a shameless shamus, or an honorable who isn't honorable.

The policeman must be a minister, a social worker, a diplomat, a tough guy and a gentleman.

And, of course, he'd have to be a genius…. because he will have to feed a family on a policeman's salary."

That is one of the most well-known poems written about police officers and I love it because it goes into great detail about what they really do.

There is also a few sayings or quotes and Bible verses that are commonly quoted with law enforcement in mind:

John 15:13 "Greater Love has none than this, that one would lay down his life for his friends."

Matthew 5:9 "Blessed are the Pacemakers, for they shall be called the children of God."

Proverbs 21:15 "When justice is done, it brings joy to the righteous but terror to the evildoers."

Romans 13:4 "For he is God's servant for your good. But if you do wrong, be afraid, for he does not bear the sword in vain. For he is the servant of God, an avenger who carries out God's wrath on the wrongdoer."

John 15:18 "If the world hates you, keep in mind that it hated me first."

Isaiah 6:8 "Then I heard the voice of the Lord saying, 'Who shall I send? And who will go for us?' And I said, 'Here am I. Send Me."

Luke 1:79 "To shine on those living in darkness and in the shadow of death, to guide our feet into the path of peace."

Isaiah 1:17 "Learn to do right; seek justice. Defend the oppressed. Take up the cause of the fatherless; plead the case of the widow."

Here are some quotes:

"Evil is powerless when the Good is not afraid."
-Former President, Ronald Reagan

"Fear is a Reaction; Courage is a Decision."
-Former UK Prime Minister, Winston Churchill

I held an interview with two of my School Resource Officers-those are the officers that protect your school because I don't want you to just take my word for it. I'm just a high school kid that knows a good bit about law enforcement but I wanted you to hear from actual Officers. I want you to know what they had to say because this is their job. This is what they had to say about what it means to be a law enforcement officer.

Question; What does it mean to be a Law Enforcement Officer?

"Ah, well that's an interesting question, I think it can go to a lot of different things. I think they are Service to the public; I think there is Protection in that, Service to Enforcing the Laws, and setting examples for others is a big part of it, and keeping the community safe and being out and getting involved in things that not many people think about getting involved in. But I think it all orients around service.

Then, going into a school resource officer, you think about kids, and I say, 'Young Men and Young

Women', it becomes more intricate. Officer Stewart has been Policing a very long time, so he is bringing his knowledge and stuff and mentoring kids, and it's really even more critical, you know, starting kids in the right direction. And that's it in a Nutshell."

-Officer Surowiec, SRO GCSP

"I think a Law Enforcement Officer spans across a broad spectrum of things. It can be really specific or it can be very broad. But in general, the pour of all Law Enforcement Officers, despite whatever special relationship you have, is, as Officer Surowiec said, is to protect and try to make the community a better place overall, leave it better than when you started into the service. That should be the general goal of any law enforcement officer. But enforcing laws is definitely one of the main things that we do as law enforcement officers and at the same time making sure that you have the right intent, the right part behind your actions. That's my say."

-Officer Stewart, SRO GCSP

They both talked about having to do with protecting the community, making it a safe place, and mentoring kids as SROs. Along with my SROs, I also turned to ask people from social media. These are civilians that wanted a say in what they thought a law enforcement officer was.

"They're men and women who serve the nation as best as they can."

-Anonymous (Instagram)

The next thing I asked was why they chose to be law enforcement officers as their career.

Question: Why did you choose to be a Law Enforcement Officer?

"I guess when I started it was a, to be honest, when I started in college and I got interested, I got good grades in it. I was like, 'This really interests me', all the aspects of it. And then when I got at it with the Police Department, the job was exciting, as a young person, and then being able to help people, and take bad guys to jail, it was awesome. And then there's just so many other aspects of it; S.W.A.T. and other things that just kind of were a lot of fun to learn about and just do. And then here in this chapter for me personally, now, it's being around the kids and mentoring the kids and maybe shaping in another direction, a positive direction.'

-Officer Surowiec, SRO GCSP

"For me, I wasn't real certain about what I wanted to do. Whenever I started in Law Enforcement, I had a close friend of mine who was a Marshall, and he, I was 19 at the time, he told me about the job opportunity working the Hall County Sheriff's Office, you began as a jailer, you were there for a couple of years, then they would send you to the academy to become a Certified Peace Officer. So really, I contemplated, maybe law enforcement, maybe education, being a teacher, those were the two things I thought about doing and the opportunity arose, I started and once it started it became one of those things that you just keep going and keep going.

The longer I was there I found more parts that interested me, getting to the academy was a huge goal of mine, and they finally sent me and I graduated the academy right when I turned 21. I was ready and I wanted to do patrol, S.W.A.T. Stuff that would give me different experiences, and then as I've gotten older and had kids I was like, okay, let's shift my direction to what I want to focus on now, so working in schools has been, my last three years I've been with hall county school so I've been with schools for about eight years now."

-Officer Stewart, SRO GCSP

Weldon

What is the Main Issue?

There is more than one main issue. Three separate parts add up together and create chaos. First up I have two words, Police Brutality. Even as someone that supports Law Enforcement, I agree that police brutality is real and it is horrible. Police brutality makes all cops look bad and causes the biggest part of the issue. Now, I also want others to understand that not every event that seems wrong is. There is a term that we use, "Lawful but Awful". This means that 'Yes, while it is horrible(awful) to do something, that does not make it illegal'. For example, if someone broke into your house and tried to kill you, and you fought back and the intruder ended up dying, you did everything by the books. Legally that would be justified. While killing someone is bad you did it because you were fearing for your safety and it would be legal.

The next part of the main issue is what we call, "Overreacting". When something happens, people explode. They jump to conclusions, 'Oh the cops shot him because he is black', is a great example. That is not always the case, maybe this person that the cop shot had a deadly weapon and tried to hurt someone. People tend to jump to conclusions and that causes overreaction and misjudgment. These reactions can cause an uproar of wrong information and then fake news spreads causing even more chaos.

And the last part of our main issue is opinions. People are entitled to their own opinions and beliefs and we need to respect that. If someone does not support the police, even though I do, I still respect them. If everyone understood that concept then we just solved a third of our problem. The issue of opinions comes up when someone tries to push their opinion as fact. Opinion ad Fact are two contradicting words, you cannot have something be both an opinion and a fact. For example, Ice Cream, a fact about ice cream is that it is a dairy product, an opinion about ice cream is that mint chocolate chip is the best flavor. Ice cream being dairy will never be an opinion because it is a fact, and ice cream flavors will always be opinions because there are multiple flavors that everyone likes differently. The same thing applies in real life. Facts do not and cannot equal Opinions. Facts do not care about your feelings. If you do not like the facts, I am sorry, but they are the facts.

Combined, these three parts make up the big issue. Police Brutality makes cops look bad, Over Reacting makes chaos, and Pushing Opinions makes Over Reacting possible and dangerous. The sad fact is that no matter how hard we try; these three problems will always be around causing pain and suffering. People need to do research before jumping to conclusions and causing a mass freak-out.

Under the main three parts of our main issue, we have multiple sections that branch off of each part. While I did not include this issue with the main issues, it is my belief that Main Stream Media is the biggest issue. A little fact, the media does not care about what really happened, they only care about what gets them more clicks and views and higher ratings. Even if that means throwing innocent people under the bus, they will. You can never trust a news outlet, always do your research, piece together the full story, find out the truth. Officer Stewart touched on this subject during our interview, here is what he had to say,

"One thing that's always bothered me a lot is the perception in general of the media and from the media or public in general.", and

"Media just really zeroing in on certain portions or incidents that have happened and not telling the whole, full story."

Weldon

Case Laws

What exactly is case law? Case law is "The law as established by the outcome of former cases". In a more understandable way, case law is a law created by the court system due to prior cases. An example is "Penn v. Mimms", the law states, by law, if an officer asks you to step out of your car you must or you can go to jail. So, no matter what you think, when asked to get out of your car by a cop there is a law saying that you have to. There are multiple case laws and "Penn v. Mimms" is a great example.

Back to my interview with my School Resource Officers, one of my questions was directed towards case laws.

Question: What case laws should everyone familiarize themselves with?

"Anything to do with search and seizure. (I put my input there and mentioned Terry v Ohio), one of many. Like I said, there's all the search and seizure aspect of stuff, anytime we take away people's rights, 1st, 2nd, 5th, we take away your amendments when we make an arrest, as the public and people should know, that's a huge responsibility to know what your rights are."

-Officer Surowiec, SRO GCSP

"I fully agree, search and seizure should be at the forefront because you are restricting another person's rights to continue living freely in a country whenever you seize them. For officers and the general public, you should certainly know your rights for whenever you do need to stop, and you do need to comply and listen to an officers orders, and the officer needs to understand when they actually have the authority to stop you or if it's a consensual encounter, you know, whenever you say, 'Hey how are you doing' and talking for a minute, there's a difference in having an articulable reasonable suspicion for an officer to initiate contact to stop that person from leaving and them just being able to go. I think the general public should know the difference between those as well as the officer should.

Aside from that, one thing that I always find comical to some degree is Miranda, that, 'You didn't read me my rights.' I wish the general public would realize that we actually don't have to read them those rights unless we are questioning them. That's one that I wish everybody would be educated on."

-Officer Stewart, SRO GCSP

There are also multiple reasons for case laws. There are case laws about traffic infractions, shootings, self-defense, etc. Even as a civilian, case laws are important to understand and know because they help you understand your rights better and help you stay safe. Case laws are not just for civilians, if you are a law enforcement officer or plan on becoming one, they can help you do your job better because you can act more rationally when you understand what the law limits you to do.

There is also Common Law, these are your typical 'Wear your seatbelt' or 'no speeding' laws. Most of everyone knows what the most common laws are and tend to follow them. People breaking common law and causing an incident is what creates new case laws. You should also familiarize yourself with these laws as they can also be helpful. Knowing your laws can benefit you in all areas of life from a simple traffic stop to self-defense when someone attacks you.

Weldon

Police Brutality

As I stated earlier, police brutality is an ongoing issue. I understand that there will be bad cops out there. But understand that not all of them are going to be bad. The first incident that I will go over is an amazing example of what not to do as a cop, and that is George Floyd. Everyone knows about this case and what happened but I'm going to break it down a little deeper.

On May 25, 2020, George Perry Floyd Jr. was being detained in Minneapolis for attempted use of a counterfeit 20-dollar bill. He was at a business trying to pay with a fake 20-dollar bill when the worker noticed it was fake and notified the Minneapolis Police Department. Several officers arrived on the scene and started an investigation when Floyd attempted to elude officers. The MPD officers then chased him a short distance and got him on the ground and in handcuffs. An officer then proceeded to kneel on George Floyd's neck for approximately 8 minutes and 46 seconds. Ignoring all complaints of shortness of breath and statements like, "I can't breathe", the officer sat there and did nothing. Due to a lack of oxygen and lack of blood to the brain, George Floyd passed away on the scene in the custody of the MPD.

Now, what exactly went wrong here? For starters, everything. There were wrong-doings on both sides of the table. George Floyd should have never tried to use a counterfeit bill; he should have never run from the officers. Then at the same time, the MPD officers should not have knelt on Floyd's neck for almost 9 minutes. It is common sense, as well as, taught to police recruits at the academy, not to kneel on someone's neck for this very reason.

There are two ways you can categorize police brutality. First, you can go by speech. In all honesty, this is a horrible category to go by. Just because an officer says something that made you mad does not mean that it is police brutality. Just like every other citizen, officers have constitutional rights including the freedom of speech as defined in the First Amendment. The second and final way is by action. This is the category you should always pay attention to. Also take into note that just because the officer does something, does not mean it is police brutality. Officers hold a set of powers that most citizens do not understand, and think are unfair. For example, an officer can carry a weapon in a weapon-free zone on or off duty.

One of the main reasons you need to familiarize yourself with laws, and your rights are so that you can understand what is, and what isn't police brutality. I have come to find that most people who say, "I know my rights", during a police interaction really have no idea what their rights are. You mainly see this when the case law Penn v Mimms comes up. Officers ask a suspect to step out of their vehicle and the suspect says, "I don't have to step out, it's my car and I don't have to get out." Well, in reality, Supreme Court Case Law 'Penn v Mimms' states that you actually do.

During the classes that I take on subjects such as Police Brutality, the instructors ingrain into the students' brains that police brutality exists. They want us to understand that it is real and it is bad. I openly support law enforcement everywhere I go and have been called many things for it. I've been called; Racist, Bootlicker, Xenophobic, Pig Food, Retarded, Stupid, Useless lump of Cells, that is just a handful of what I have been called. I say that to make a point, just because you support law enforcement does not make you any of those things. Don't let people and their attitudes towards you affect the way you feel.

During the interview with my school resource officers, one of the subjects I brought up was police brutality and what they thought about when they heard those words.

Question: What comes to mind when you think about Police Brutality?

"Well, thinking about it, I would take the word 'Police' out of it. Any brutality in any profession against something is not good. And I think we're, personally in my profession and any profession there are bad apples, and that goes without saying anything. We're very fortunate in Gwinnett County and the school system we have a very professional department where nothing like that is a ramped thing, it's not like an everyday thing, which is fortunate. But unfortunately, being a police officer, we are encountered by, often we do things, reactions to people that are trying to hurt somebody or something else, in that stance, we don't have a choice, sometimes, it is what it is. We try to do it professionally and to the best that we can."

-Officer Surowiec, SRO GCSP

"Yeah, I think, when I think of police brutality, the first thing that comes to mind really is media. Media just really zeroing in on certain portions or incidents that have happened and not telling the whole, full story, and not revealing the whole, full background behind what happened. Which can create a problem, because, if you're focused on one portion of the event and you don't see what led up to it and why the officer is doing what he is doing, then you can't truly understand what's going on, you just see the bad part that is ugly.

Now beyond that, there are certainly instances where officers do go too far and have gone too far, and those officers give the rest of us a bad name and paint us with a broad brush and make us look like bad guys as well. And as Officer Surowiec said, I always try to tell everybody that brutality in a specific case is that, don't want me in with it, don't group us as a whole with it, because, there are bad teachers, there are bad lawyers, there are bad doctors, there are people who make mistakes and do bad things in every single profession in this world, and just because we wear a uniform and look the same doesn't mean we're the same as another person wearing the same uniform."

-Officer Stewart, SRO GCSP

Again, along with the SROs, I brought in other people with different perspectives to interview. This next answer to our last question is the one that stuck out to me the most other than the SRO answers.

"When police are abusing power and it's been proven there wasn't a good reason to do so."

-Anonymous (Instagram)

Weldon

Use of Force

The use of force is a huge part of law enforcement that is overlooked by the public. It is also very confusing to understand unless you study it. Use of force and the use of force continuum outline what the rules to using force are. From a taser to a gun, these rules are used to dictate if what happened was lawful. Back to case laws, there are three main case laws used to define the use of force. You should also familiarize yourself with these case laws as they can help you in the future if anything happens to you.

Supreme Court Case '*Graham v. Connor*', 490 U.S. 386 (1989): The Supreme Court ruled that excessive use of force claims must be evaluated under the "objectively reasonable" standard of the Fourth Amendment, which requires courts to consider the facts and circumstances surrounding an officer's use of force rather than the intent or motivation of an officer during that use of force.

Supreme Court Case '*Tennessee v. Garner*', 471 U.S. 1 (1985): A civil case in which the Supreme Court of the United States held that, under the Fourth Amendment, when a law enforcement officer is pursuing a fleeing suspect, the officer may not use deadly force to prevent escape unless "the officer has probable cause to believe that the suspect poses a significant threat of death or serious physical injury to the officer or others."

Supreme Court Case '*Terry v. Ohio*', 392 U.S. 1 (1968): A landmark decision of the Supreme Court of the United States in which the Court ruled that it is not unconstitutional for American police to "stop and frisk" a person they reasonably suspect to be armed and involved in a crime.

These are the three main supreme court rulings that are associated with the use of force. There are plenty more minor case laws that I will not go over, you can find them online.

Graham v Connor is the case that outlines what we consider excessive use of force. It entails what actions are excessive use of force and also when those actions may be allowed. The rules that are set from case law are very tight-knit and not easy to get around, nor are they ignored.

Tennessee v Garner is the case that outlines the rules when it comes to using deadly force such as a firearm. It outlines when you are and are not allowed to use this force. When a suspect is fleeing an officer may not use deadly force unless that officer has reason to believe the suspect is a threat to others.

Terry v Ohio is the case that outlines the rules that apply to a stop of any kind. Whether it's a traffic stop or a walking stop, these rules apply. A 'Stop and Frisk', or 'Terry Stop' is when an officer stops you and does a non-thorough search of your persons. During a Stop and Frisk stop, officers cannot just brag around your pockets, that cannot go into your pockets, all they can do is pat-down, no grabbing. If, while patting you down, the officer feels what is like a weapon, they can full search and now go into your pockets and find out what they felt.

As stated earlier, Use of Force is confusing when you don't know it. If you are a law enforcement officer or want to become one, I suggest that you study the use of force.

In the use of force, there is a continuum. This use of force continuum states that an officer should always have the next step up of force compared to the suspect. If the suspect has a heavy metal stick, you should use your gun, heavy metal sticks can be deadly weapons. If a suspect has a knife, first try a taser and if that doesn't work then you should exceed to using a firearm. The continuum goes along the lines of five levels; Professional, Tactical, Threshold, Harmful, Lethal.

The professional level is no force needed and everyone is calm and cooperative. The Tactical level is when they start mouthing back at you and indicating that they want to not cooperate. The threshold level is when they go physical and start fighting with their hands. The Harmful level of force is when the suspect has a weapon and makes threats to use it. And last, the Lethal level is when they do use their weapon and cause serious injury to a person or officer near the suspect.

Along with learning the use of force, you should also take self-defense classes and defensive tactics courses. I cannot stress enough to you that these can save your life! Learning to fight and defend yourself can come in handy on multiple occasions.

One big issue currently with the use of force subject is, do law enforcement officials need to have firearms? I asked some people on Instagram and this is by far my favorite answer.

"Yes but clearly more of a background check or training.
-@shanetc1146 (Instagram)

That is one of the main points I try to bring up is that, sometimes, our officers need more training. When I talk about Fund or Defund the police later, I will go over that topic in more detail.

Fund or Defund the Police

A huge part of this ongoing debate is people saying that we should defund the police. Defunding the police does not just mean that we take the money and funding away from them, we also use that money for another area of the community. There are some pros and mostly cons about this idea though.

Sure, defunding the police might give us more money to spend on education, maybe the money is very helpful in another part of the community. I understand where these people are coming from. All they see is the news and want to defund police and fund maybe a daycare. I understand that it does sound like a great idea. Help the public out and put money towards what some people say is more important.

But on the other hand, people are also pushing for police reform, they want better officers, they want the officers to have more training. The issue is that if we defund the police, how are we going to pay for that reform, how are we going to pay for better training when we don't have the money to do so?

People who want to both, defund the police, and want police reform, are contradictory to both of those statements. You cannot take money away from departments and then ask for better training when they don't have the money to get better training. That is why this is one of the most debated topics when it comes to policing.

Another part of this argument is that they just need the money because they don't ever use it all, that is just a straight-up lie. The truth is, police departments are already underfunded as it is, they already lack the funding for the best training possible. This is also a great reason to explain why some of these incidents that happened over the past few years did. Most of the officers from many departments that have many shootings are undertrained. With less training, an officer is less likely to act; professionally, Calm, and Rationally during a high-stress event. Officers with more training can better handle a situation because they know what they are doing and are confident in their abilities. This leads to police needing more funding.

So again, at first glance, defunding the police seems like a great idea, but then, looking more deeply into it, not so much. I completely agree that our education system needs more funding, but also with that, you would need protection. I would rather be safe and uneducated than be scared for my safety and smart.

Public Perception

A huge part of how law enforcement is looked at is public perception. This is the term used to describe what the media might say all the way to how an officer conducts himself. For example, take two officers. One officer has a cleanly pressed and ironed uniform that fits him well and shines his boots and is cleanly shaved. The second officer has an oversized uniform, it's all wrinkled, scuffs all over his boots, and has a scruff-looking beard and uncut hair. Which officer looks better? Which officer would you choose to protect you? I personally would choose the first officer because the public perception is that, he looks good so he must know what he is doing. I would definitely choose the more professional-looking officer.

The way you present yourself is one of the most important things in policing even though it might seem like the smallest minor detail. From having a crease in your pants to shining your boots. Present yourself like you want others to see you. If you want to look like you are at the top of your game, iron your uniform, shine your boots, make sure your nametag and badge are pinned on straight, polish your metal uniform accessories such as a nametag, badge, or belt buckle. Every little detail matters.

Weldon

Leadership

Leadership is the basis of every law enforcement agency I have seen. What exactly is a leader? How can I trust what you say about being a leader? Those are both questions you might be asking me right now. I believe I am qualified to speak on leadership because of my background and accomplishments. I have completed multiple leadership courses and hold many leadership positions. I am a law enforcement explorer, that takes leadership. I am an officer in the Air Force JROTC program. In order to become an officer in AF-JROTC you first need to pass the Cadet Leadership School which is the equivalent to OCS of the military. I am the Armed Regulation Drill Team Commander and have been awarded multiple awards such as the Air Commando Association National Award, Certificate of Excellence for Outstanding Cadet, Certificate of Excellence for Superior Performance, as well as the Cadet Leadership School awards.

Now that you have those in mind, I believe I am qualified to speak about leadership. What is a leader? A leader is one who knows the way, Goes the way, and shows the way. As a leader you must know what you are doing, how can you do something without even knowing what it is. Not only do you need to know what to do, but you must also follow through and actually do the task.

But here is the kicker that separates a real leader from a boss. Not only do you need to know what to do and do it, but you also need to show others how to do it so they can succeed as well. A boss is someone who tells you what to do and sends you off to do it by yourself, a leader tells you what to do and goes off to help you do it because they want you to succeed. "Good leaders become great not because of their power, but because of their ability to empower others." -John Maxwell.

There are eleven principles of leadership: Know yourself and seek self-improvement, be technically and tactically proficient, develop a sense of responsibility of those under you, make sound and timely decisions, set an example, know those under you and look out for them, keep those under you informed, seek responsibility and take responsibility for your actions, ensure task assigned are understood, supervised, and accomplished, help those under you excel, and put qualified people on the task relating to their abilities.

Know yourself and seek self-improvement. If you are a leader, you must humble yourself and understand that you don't know everything. If you don't know something, ask for help and educate yourself to become better. Don't lie to the people you are put over because that takes out of the integrity aspect. Remember, great leaders, surround themselves with people that are smarter than them.

Be technically and tactically proficient. As a leader, you should be qualified for the position you hold. Don't apply for a position you know nothing about. You need to be proficient in every way possible that relates to your position.

Develop a sense of responsibility for those under you. You need to be able to take the blame when something turns out the way it should not have, even if you had no part in it. As a leader, you are in charge of the people below you which means that you are in charge of making sure everything goes as planned. If one person that you are in charge of, even if you did not do anything, you are still responsible because you must ensure that what they are doing is right.

Make sound and timely decisions. When you are put over people, they depend on you. You need to be able to make a decision quickly but also the right decision. This principle ties into our technically and tactically proficiency.

Set an Example. Do you want the people you are in charge of to act unprofessionally? Do you want them to act inappropriately? The answer should be no. One big way that people under you get their personality and attitude is by you, their superior. Set an example and act accordingly to what you are supposed to. Follow the rules, conduct yourself professionally.

Know those under you and look out for them. Looking back to the principle of setting an example, this ties into that. Get to know that people you are over because having a professional relationship and knowing who you are working with can make working with them easier. Look out for the people under you, as I stated earlier, they look up to you. If you look out for them and protect them, then they will succeed.

Keep those under you informed. Have you ever had someone put in charge of you and they did absolutely nothing? Give out important information as soon as you can. Explain the information you have. Do not hold back anything from your inferiors because they might see that as something negative.

Seek and take responsibility for your actions. Not only do you need to assume responsibility for those under you, but you must also do it for yourself. No one wants a leader over them that is a liar and does not own up to their own actions.

Ensure tasks assigned are understood, supervised, and accomplished. Thoroughly explain every important detail of a task to your people. Watch and spectate over them while they perform as well as provide any help they might need. Make sure what needs to get done, gets done.

Help those under you excel. When one of your team members is struggling, provide the help and training they need. If you let the people you are put over fail, then you too have failed.

Put qualified people on a task that corresponds with their abilities. If you have a team member that is skilled in negotiation, do not put them on a tech support station, make them a negotiator. Do not set yourself and your team up for failure.

Weldon

Not Politics

One thing that bugs me is that this 'Police v Anti-Police' debate always gets turned political, It's not. Choosing one of these sides does not make you a republican, democrat, conservative, or liberal. While you can argue that people that support police tend to identify as conservative republicans or that people who do not support them identify as liberal democrats, it is not up to a political party, it is up to your free will.

I personally know and have met people who claim to be democrats and liberals that support the police. I have run into republicans and conservatives that do not support them. I have also had run-ins with people who do not affiliate with any political party and they have their own opinions as well.

This is not a political debate!

Weldon

Thin Blue Line

The thin blue line is a symbol of honor and respect in the law enforcement community. It often gets mixed up with the term 'Blue Lives Matter' but understand they are different. The thin blue line is typically depicted by a plain black space with a blue line running through the middle of it from left to right. The top black part represents calm and safety. It represents being safe. The bottom black part represents chaos and crime. It is about the evil and bad in the world. The blue line running across that separates the two represents the law enforcement officers that keep us safe. The line represents the divide between crime and justice.

There are other versions of the thin blue line that you might run across. One that you will likely see the most is a black and white American flag with a single blue stripe below the canton. The canton is where the stars are located. You might also see a spartan military helmet and shield with a blue line running from top to bottom.

The thin blue line and the saying 'Blue Lives Matter' are two very different things. While yes, they both are typically used in the support of law enforcement you might be surprised with what they are. The thin blue line again represents the divide between chaos and calm.

The saying 'Blue Lives Matter' is a retaliation against the saying 'Black Lives Matter'.

The thin blue line originates from the British Infantry Regiment in 1854. The original term was 'The Thin Red Line' referring to the red uniforms of the British infantry. It is not clearly known when the term was used for law enforcement rather than the military. There is a 'Thin Green Line' flag used to represent the military as well.

All in all, the thin blue line symbol is not the same as the 'Blue Lives Matter' movement. It represents chaos and peace. It represents the people that hold the line between chaos and peace.

Blue Lives Matter

The saying 'Blue Lives Matter' has many meanings behind it. It can be used to combat the saying of 'Black Lives Matter' but it is the name of a movement created in 2014.

The Blue Lives Matter movement was created on December 20, 2014, after the ambush murders of Officers Rafael Ramos and Wenjian Liu. The movement was established in New York City as a countermovement that advocates for law enforcement and the crimes committed against them.

The movement inspired the highly criticized state law in Louisiana that made it a hate crime to target; law enforcement officers, firefighters, and emergency medical first responders.

Criticisms against the movement bring things up such as 'Black lives are always under threat whereas police are never under threat'. Do as you please with that information. Some law enforcement officers are against this law as well. The reason being, this law could make resisting arrest a hate crime.

The website, formerly known as bluelivesmatter.blue, now the policetribune.com is a media source for law enforcement related news.

Weldon

Black Lives Matter

Black Lives Matter is a movement that is dedicated to social and racial justice. They claimed to advocate against police brutality and any racially charged crime against black people.

There are two parts to Black Lives Matter. There is first the organization, and second, the movement itself. These both have their differences and similarities. The movement itself does not associate directly with the organization but they do share similar beliefs.

These beliefs can vary from either source. Both organizations believe that there should be police reform and police defunding. Both share the belief that there should be justice for wrongful police shootings. The organization has a different view of the nuclear family. They believe that there should be no nuclear family and had that posted on their website until they started to get complaints about the claim and took it down.

Black Lives Matter began in January 2013 after the shooting death of Travon Martin in February 2012. The movement became national after the deaths of two more African American teens in 2014. In 2015 they got involved in the 2016 US Presidential Election.

The movement became very popular with 67% of adult Americans supporting the movement in 2018. Throughout the recent years though, the approval and support rates dropped to 55% with mainly; whites, Hispanics, and Latinos dropping off of the movement.

Black Lives Matter claimed responsibility for the largest number of protests in the United States over the past few years. While most of these protests were peaceful, some of them turned into violent riots with the help of the domestic terrorist organization, Antifa. Antifa stands for 'Anti-Fascist and is a group of people that use violence to gain political pull during election times and any major political event.

All Lives Matter

The term 'All Lives Matter' is not an actual movement. It was simply created to be a counter chant to the 'Black Lives Matter' chant. This term is used by people that are against the Black Lives Matter movement.

The saying was coined by counter-protesters at BLM protests during 2012 through current year events.

People tend to put All Lives Matter in comparison to Blue Lives Matter but again, they are very different. Not all people that support police back the 'All Lives Matter' slogan, and vice versa.

Weldon

Don't Talk About What You Don't Know

Let's get the elephant out of the room, you do not know everything. I don't know everything. We need to accept that and humble ourselves to learn new things every day. Do not pretend to know everything.

Not only does this tie into your everyday life but it also ties into not jumping to conclusions and making assumptions. Do your research, do not go off of 'oh I saw that so it must be true.' Do not listen to people simply because of their fame, famous people can be wrong too.

I myself am guilty of making up fake information. I know people who were personally impacted by their decision to lie about important information. This applies to lying to get out of trouble as well. Only speak on subjects you are qualified to speak on.

Weldon

War on Police

Whether or not you want to believe the war on police is real, it is. Ambush attacks and shootings targeted at law enforcement officers have spiked tremendously over the past two years alone. Law enforcement officers have been targeted for simply doing their job.

Officers that are not even involved in the shootings of unarmed subjects are being targeted. Innocent officers are being targeted. These officers, just like you, have a family. They must provide for their family off of a law enforcement salary. They have husbands and wives, sons and daughters, and pets. They have people that love and care for them and they get targets pinned on their heads for doing their job.

The main issue here is that innocent law enforcement professionals are being sought after in a bad way. There have been roughly 73 officers killed in the line of duty due to ambush and assaults from Jan 2021-Sep 2021 as compared to the 66 total in the whole year of 2018 and the even lower 60 in total killed in 2015. As you can see, the numbers keep rising. In 2020, we saw the highest record-breaking law enforcement death by assault and ambushes at 74 officers killed in the line of duty.

Weldon

Felony and High-Risk Traffic Stops

The reason I bring Felony(FTS) and High-Risk Vehicle Stops(HRVS) into this book is because they are commonly misunderstood by the public. FTS and HRVS are done with more aggression because the reason they are done is more serious. For example, if I run a license tag and the owner of the vehicle has a warrant out for their arrest for ADW(Assault with a Deadly Weapon), I would use more force and aggression because the person in the car is more likely than not armed and they would also more likely than not try to use that weapon against me.

When an FTS or HRVS is performed, typically the officers on scene would use their service weapons for their safety and the safety of others. This is because of the nature of the traffic stop. The officers would also be a little less lenient towards the subject in the vehicle. The commands that they give would sound more forceful.

Weldon

Lawful Commands

A lawful command is any order or command given to you by a law enforcement officer. These can be as simple as "keep your hands where I can see them" to "get out of the vehicle" and a serious as "drop the weapon".

These commands tie into case laws such as Pennsylvania V Mimms with a command like "Can you please step out of the vehicle for me?"

I don't have the best explanation for lawful commands but what I can say is, if a police officer tells you to do something, do it(Unless it puts your life at risk). Even if it seems crazy, do it, then fight it in court and the officer would get in trouble and you would be compensated for what happened.

Weldon

Fight in the Courts

Something often said about policing is to fight in the courts, not on the streets. This means that instead of resisting arrest or arguing with the officer, go along with it, and then you can fight back with fewer to no repercussions in the courts.

This is because it is safer for you and everyone involved to do it that way. Not only is it safer, but it also is faster.

If you get pulled over and the officer asked you to step out of your car, and you refuse, you can get charged with extra charges like resisting arrest, failure to comply, disobeying a lawful order, and so on. Just get out of your car and listen to what the officer says.

Most officers don't want to hurt you, cause harm to you, or harass you, they simply are doing their job. Disobeying an order from an officer will just rack up more charges that can get pinned on you.

Also, unless you actually know your rights, and have taken classes, and have certifications when it comes to the law, do NOT say "I don't have to do that, I know my rights.". Something I have found is that people that say, "I know my rights", typically don't.

What They Deal With

On a daily basis, law enforcement officers encounter many different types of people. They might run into a complete stranger, someone that they have never met. Maybe, they would run into someone that they might have met once or twice, and sometimes, they run into people they know personally.

Apart from the way they know people, they have to deal with the way these people act. They might pull someone over for having a broken taillight and they just wanted to let the person know, but the person is completely rude and disrespectful to the officer when all he was trying to do was let them know that the taillight was out.

Sometimes they might run into someone who is the nicest person ever. Someone might have just committed armed robbery and still be 100 percent respectful and compliant. People are weird, and these officers have to deal with that every day that they go to work.

Before you go on and say "oh well they should have done that" or "Nah, that's not possible." understand that anything can and will happen. Go on a ride-along, most agencies in the U.S. require you to be 18 or older to do one and they are a great experience. They help give you an insight into what the officers have to deal with on a daily basis.

Not only do officers deal with people, but they also deal with trauma and work on cases that would keep you up at night. Officers respond to homicides, they respond to car accidents, they really do a lot more than law. They see things that are horrific and unseeable. Dealing with anything medical like on a motor vehicle accident scene is difficult without the right training.

Some people can not bear to see blood or any broken bones and get nauseous and might pass out. Some people do not know how to deal with medical treatment. But, sometimes, if an officer is first on scene and arrives before medical, they might need to provide whatever care they can.

You really need to step into their shoes to understand what they deal with all the time. Put that into consideration before you say anything because they go through things that you couldn't fathom.

Thank You

I just wanted to give a huge thank you to those who participated in lending a piece of their mind to put in this book. Not only that, but I wanted to thank you, the reader, for taking the time to read my work, that means a lot to me.

I hope you feel better about these topics than you did before reading, I hope I gave you the information you needed to choose a side or just to learn more.

Please check out my podcast: "What's New?" on; YouTube, Apple Podcast, Spotify, and Google Podcast.

Before you go, keep this in mind, Psalm 23:4a- Though I walk through the valley of the shadow of death, I will fear no evil.

Take that as a reminder to stay vigilant, to watch yourself, and to expect deception so you are never deceived, do not let others bring you down. Stay Frosty, stay Safe, until next time...

Weldon

About the Author

Zachary Weldon is a Law Enforcement Explorer in the metro Atlanta area in Georgia. He has firearms training and is currently working on his Emergency Medical Response(EMR) Certification.

He attends a Gwinnett County High School, and is a part of the Air Force Junior ROTC program. He has completed the Cadet Leadership Course and is an officer in the program.

At the time he started working on this project he was 15 years old and was not sure whether or not he wanted to actually attempt to publish the book or if he just wanted to work on it for fun.

After he graduates high school, he plans on attending the University of North Georgia and joining the Corps of Cadets then commissioning as an officer into the United States Army.

www.ingramcontent.com/pod-product-compliance
Lightning Source LLC
Chambersburg PA
CBHW070757250726
48662CB00004B/1852